Table of Contents

What is SEO and why do I need it?

A foundational part of any ecommerce marketing strategy should be **Search Engine Optimization**, or **SEO**. By doing SEO, you can be found by your potential customers from search engines like Google, Yahoo, and Bing. Your website would show up in the search results when people search for things that you sell or provide information about.

What is SEO, then, you might ask?

SEO is the sum total of all the activities and techniques that help position your website in such a way that it ranks high in search engines.

SEO is crucial because it is *free, qualified traffic coming to your website*. You don't need to pay to be found in Google. You just have to provide *helpful, valuable, and relevant* content that answers the questions that people are asking.

A lot of ecommerce stores are completely killing it when it comes to SEO - in fact, they are so well-positioned that they don't do any other form of inbound marketing *except* SEO - they get tens if not hundreds of thousands of buying customers coming to their ecommerce store through search engines - and the best part about it is that it is all FREE TRAFFIC!

FREE?!

Well, not exactly. While the traffic itself is free, you have to invest a lot of time and sometimes money before your online store has enough value and content that search engines rank it high for certain terms.

The time and financial investment that you will put into your SEO efforts will be of three types:

1. Keyword research
2. On-page SEO
3. Off-page SEO

Keywords are word or phrases that people type in the search box on Google. Keywords are the foundation of search engine optimization, and they are the first step in finding out whether or not people are actually looking for your product or information to start with! There is no SEO without keyword research.

Luckily for us, there are many ways to find out keywords and to see whether they are in demand or not, and we will get into that in the first section.

On-page SEO is the content and information that you place on your website itself. What the page's title is, what the headings are, how long the content is, how valuable the content is, and whether or not it is about what people are looking for.

On-page SEO is also about how you link one page to another on your website itself. The pages you optimize include your home page, category pages, product pages, information pages, and blog posts.

Off-page SEO is largely the links that your content earns or the links that you build(or other people create) to your content. A link you earn is where someone links to you because they found your content and they liked it.

A link you build is where you either ask someone to place a link to your site from theirs, or you write an article or a blog post for another website and link to your website from it.

These are only two of many ways to build links to your store, but on the whole, off-page SEO is how you network and build awareness for your store elsewhere on the internet.

This book focuses on SEO specifically for eCommerce stores.

For this reason, we won't go into too much detail about the more technical side of SEO. To keep things simple, this book is split up into those three things: keyword research, on-page SEO, and off-page SEO - all from the perspective of someone specifically looking to grow their ecommerce stores.

Some key terms you need to know

Traffic that comes to your website by being found in search engine results is called *organic* traffic. Other was to drive traffic are advertising, which is called *paid* traffic, or by having other websites link to you and people finding you by clicking on those links, which is called *referral* traffic. If people come to your site by directly typing in the address, it is called *direct* traffic. If someone comes to your site from social media networks, it is called *social* traffic.

Generally, your traffic should be a healthy mix of organic, referral, and direct traffic. If you do paid advertising, then there will be some paid traffic in the mix as well.

Authority is how valuable your site is perceived to be on a particular subject. Moz, for example, is considered an authority site on SEO. Anything they publish related to SEO and marketing gets a boost from being on their domain, and gets an instant boost in the search engine rankings. **Your goal with SEO should be to build *authority* for your ecommerce store.**

A *link* is a bit of code on a website that makes certain text or images clickable - when you click on it, you "jump" from that page to the page that the code points to. It's called a "link" because it joins one page to another.

Indexing is the process through which search engines visit your website, see what's in it, and add it to their index, or database. Then, according to their algorithm, they will show whichever sites from their index they feel are most relevant to that particular search query.

Three kinds of SEO

Broadly speaking, SEO is of three types: *white-hat*, *grey-hat*, and *black-hat*.

White-hat SEO is fully legitimate SEO, following Google's rules and suggestions(mostly) to the letter. This is the *proper* way to get your site ranked, and it requires lots of hard work, networking, and relationship-building. This is what you should use to build businesses, as you will be safe in the long run.

Grey-hat SEO is a mix between following the rules and bending them. You can take some shortcuts here and there, and this will be a mix of legit

SEO and shady stuff. You shouldn't rely *only* on grey-hat SEO for a business, but it can be used to add a little jolt when other things are dry.

Black-hat SEO is the SEO underworld. Here, you use software to spin hundreds of versions of the same article, blast those to automated websites, create 1000s of social links on automated accounts, and the works. This is for getting sites to rank quickly - but they will get removed from Google's index just as quickly, too. So these are *churn-and-burn* sites - not a good way to rank a long-lasting business.

Everything I cover here is white-hat SEO, with a little bit of grey-hat mixed in.

A quick note on how search engines think

Whether or not a particular page ranks for a certain keyword depends on two factors - the authority of the *domain* and the authority of the page itself. So a page on Amazon.com has a lot of weight because it has Amazon's authority backing it, but if the *page itself does not have any authority, it can be outranked with some work.*

Also, SEO is a long-term game. You can't expect to have rankings within a week. If you have a brand new website, expect at least 3 to 6 months before you start seeing some significant search traffic - it's just how much time this process requires.

SEO is a continuous process. It's not something that's done and left be. If you become complacent, someone else will be waiting to outrank you.

Of course, once you get big enough, you'll start earning links and such naturally, so things will get easier - but until then, most of it is a very manual process.

At this point, I know you must be dying to dive right in! But there is one last thing that we must cover before getting into it.

Keeping track

Before you embark on your SEO campaign, it's important to have a way to measure and keep track of what's going on!

Here are a couple of things you need to set up.

Google Analytics

Google Analytics is a must-have for any website. It's powerful and best of all, completely free. This is the best way to track how much traffic you are getting and where you are getting it from.

The data you will get from Google Analytics will also help you in doing more SEO in the future. To cover all aspects of Google Analytics would require another whole book, but we'll cover a few of the main screens you can utilize.

To install Google Analytics, you'll have to head over to http://www.google.com/analytics

Sign in with your Google account, and you'll be walked through a series of steps to set up your account.

In the "New Account" screen, you'll be first presented with whether you want to set up for a website or a mobile app. Choose website.

Next, fill out the form. The first field will be for Account name - this is the main "folder" so to speak, and in it will be multiple websites. Since we are only going for one at this point in time, feel free to name it whatever you like.

For my blog, for example, the account name is "Ecom Blog". This is for internal use only.

The next fields are for Website name - this again is just for internal use, so use something that you and people in your organization can remember and identify easily.

The next field is website address, followed by industry category(this helps Google process their own data better), time zone, and some checkboxes whether you would like Google to share data with their partners or not.

Click the button that says "Generate tracking code", and you'll be taken to a new page which shows you your tracking code. You need to paste this code on to each and every page that you want to track.

That sounds like quite a job, doesn't it? Luckily, most shopping carts and even WordPress make it very easy to do. You just have to paste the code in one spot, and the shopping cart or Wordpress will handle the rest for you.

If you use Shopify or Bigcommerce, they have very well documented instructions on how to implement this code. If you use Wordpress, the methods will differ, but you can use a plugin such as Yoast Google Analytics.

Yoast is particularly easy because it takes care of all the technical details for you.

Now that you have Google Analytics installed, you can access it anytime by heading over to http://www.google.com/analytics.

Whenever you open Google Analytics, you'll first see the Audience screen with 30 days of data. This will be how many unique visitors, how many repeat visitors, and how many pages were viewed on your site.

You can change the date range to see whatever range you like.

There is a lot to explore in Google Analytics, but these things will give you the most insights that you need every day. For more data, you can always dig deeper in the other sections.

The **Audiences** tab which opens up when you start will show you how much time your visitors are spending on your pages. This is an important metric! The amount of time they spend on your pages should reflect how much content you have!

If you expect your audience to be spending a lot more time than they actually are, your content is not doing what it is supposed to!

Another important metric it will show is the **bounce rate**. The bounce rate is the percentage of visitors who leave your site from the page they reach without taking any other action. In other words, if someone doesn't click any other link or button and just clicks "back" directly or closes the window, that increases your bounce rate.

Bounce rate is important because Google considers it as one of its many ranking factors. The lower your bounce rate, the more relevant your site seems to be to its visitors, and the more relevant your site is to visitors, the more relevant it is to Google.

In Audiences, you can also see where your users are coming from by clicking the Geo link, and what their demographics/interests are by using those respective tabs. This data is incredibly useful for planning future content strategies(more on that later).

Note: to see demographics and interests data, you need to enable it beforehand! Once it's enabled, wait for a few weeks before you start gathering this data.

Next, I like to pop in to the **Acquisition** tab. This will show you how you got your visitors and where they came from.

Click **Acquisition**, and head over to **Source/Medium**. This will show you where the traffic came from and what kind of traffic it was - organic search, referral links, pay per click, email, social, and direct.

You can also head over to Search Engine Optimization under Acquisition and you'll be able to see limited data as to what keywords people are using to find your site. You will have to link your Google Analytics to your Google Webmaster Tools account to see this data.

Finally, under the **Behavior** link, you can see what people really do once they are on your website. Under **Site content**, you want to look at **All content**, **Landing pages**, and **Exit pages**.

All content will show you a list of whatever pages people visited on your website, along with how many times those pages were visited, what that specific pages bounce rate was, how much time people spent on that page, and how many people exited from that page.

Landing pages shows you what pages people first arrived on at your site. Landing pages is powerful because it can give you immediate feedback as to what pages you have optimized are getting how much traffic.

Finally, exit pages shows you where people are leaving from. It helps you see where your proverbial bucket is leaking.

Theres a lot more you can learn about Google Analytics from doing some more research online, but this overview should be enough to get you on your way.

Now that we have all of the basics covered, we can move on to learning about Keyword Research!

Part 1: Keyword Research

Head keywords, long tail keywords, and variants

Keywords are of three types: *head keywords, long tail keywords,* and *variants.*

Head keywords are single word or two word queries that have lots of search volume(many people are searching for that word), like "car," "laptop," or "iphone." To the untrained eye, these keywords might be the goldmines worth ranking for, since they get hundreds of thousands, if not millions of searches per month.

The problem with these keywords is that they are *insanely* competitive. There are millions of websites competing for the same keyword, and the websites ranking on the home page are giant, authoritative websites.

A search for "cars" brings up websites like Cars.com, Wikipedia, Disney(the movie), IMDb, CNET, and Amazon.com. Each of these websites has HUGE authority, and so attempting to outrank them would be like an ant trying to take on an elephant in a fight.

New **Cars**, Used **Cars**, Car Reviews | **Cars**.com
www.**cars**.com/ ▾ Cars.com ▾
Use **Cars**.com to search 2.6 million new & used **car** listings or get a dealer quote. Our
easy-to-use online tools put you a step ahead in your next vehicle ...
Buy - Advanced Search - Car Reviews - Kelley Blue Book Used-Car ...

1) PA: 89   1,337,493 links   DA: 87   Access more link metrics with PRO   Link Analysis

Cars (2006) - IMDb
www.imdb.com/title/tt0317219/ ▾ Internet Movie Database ▾
★★★★ ★ Rating: 7.3/10 - 166,727 votes
With Owen Wilson, Bonnie Hunt, Paul Newman, Larry the Cable Guy. A hot-shot race-
car named Lightning McQueen gets waylaid in Radiator Springs, where he ...
Full Cast & Crew - Trivia - Quotes - Filming Locations

2) PA: 86   3,333 links   DA: 100   Access more link metrics with PRO   Link Analysis

Cars (film) - Wikipedia, the free encyclopedia
en.wikipedia.org/wiki/**Cars**_(film) ▾ Wikipedia ▾
Cars is a 2006 American computer-animated comedy-adventure sports film produced by
Pixar Animation Studios, and directed and co-written by John Lasseter ...
Fabulous Hudson Hornet - Lightning McQueen - Cars (soundtrack) - Doc Hudson

3) PA: 48   3 links   DA: 100   Access more link metrics with PRO   Link Analysis

Disney **Cars**
cars.disney.com/ ▾ Disney.com ▾
Welcome to the Disney **Cars** homepage. Browse movies, watch videos, play games,
and meet the characters from Disney's World of **Cars**.

4) PA: 73   2,576 links   DA: 92   Access more link metrics with PRO   Link Analysis

Car Tech: **Car** technology reviews, GPS, bluetooth, hybrid **car** tech ...
reviews.cnet.com/**car**-tech/ ▾ CNET ▾
Car tech reviews and ratings, video reviews, user opinions, most popular GPS systems,
Bluetooth technology buying guides, prices, and comparisons.

5) PA: 87   89,774 links   DA: 97   Access more link metrics with PRO   Link Analysis

Next up comes two to three word keywords. These are still competitive, but not *as* competitive as one word queries. In fact, if you do your research properly, you might come across a keyword that you can actually rank for with some solid, consistent SEO. These are the kinds of keywords that you want to build your store around - some people also like to refer to this keyword as a *niche*.

I decide on whether a niche is good or not by putting it up against 15 criteria:

1.　　Potential to add value: Can you do anything with your store besides just list the products like a me-too store? If you can add value in any way - either by creating content, presenting the products in a unique way, or just differentiate yourself in some useful way, you may be on to something.

2.　　Market size: How big is your target market? Are there

enough people interested in your product or service to make you good enough money so that this venture is worth your while? You can verify how big your market is by seeing how many searches the main keyword gets per month, or how big the idea is on social media networks like Facebook, Pinterest, and Reddit.

3.   Trend: It would be terrible if you put all that effort into an online store only for the product to become obsolete in a few months. Is the trend for your product up? Find out at http://www.google.com/trends

4.   Competition: Competition is a good thing. Trust me. If nobody else is selling what you are selling, chances are not many people want it. Competition means there is a market - the pie is big and there can be a piece for everyone. Just remember to keep criteria number 1(added value potential) in mind when you study your competition.

5.   Not locally available: If the products you are looking into are difficult to source locally, then there's another plus point. Walmart and Target won't be your competitors simply because they don't have what you are selling. To find that, people have to come online. And where are you? Online.

6.   Markup and selling price: Can you get the product for cheap enough that you can sell it for a decent profit?

7.   Repeat business potential: If you are going to spend all that effort to try and get visitors to your site(SEO takes a while!) then it would be awesome if each visitor had the potential to become a repeat customer. This way your return on investment for SEO would become manifold.

8.   Size, weight, and durability: This factor isn't as highly correlated to SEO as the other factors, but it is still important. While it's just as easy or hard to rank for a store selling elephant statues as there is for a store selling something much smaller, elephant statues are much, much harder to ship. Trust me!

9.   Seasonality: This is again more about the profitability of a business rather than the SEO, but a seasonal product which only sells well for a few months a year may not be so much worth your while as a product that can sell well year-round.

10.   Turnover: Turnover is how often your product line

changes. Clothing, for example, would probably change every season, whereas something like kitchen tools would probably remain the same for a longer period of time. You'll have trouble doing SEO for high turnover products in the early stages of your business, before it has enough authority. You may find that by the time certain product pages get around to ranking, they've already gone out of production!

11.   Perishability: A product that can easily go bad may not be the wisest investment idea, since you may lose a lot of stock before you can move it, especially during the early stages of your business.

12.   Barrier to entry: How difficult is it for someone to get started in your business? If it's too easy, then there are probably way too many people out there just waiting to compete with you. If it's a little hard to get into this business, your chances of doing well are much better.

13.   Suppliers: Can you easily source your product? Where will you get it from? If you are going to drop-ship, are any suppliers willing to drop ship? Most importantly, are these suppliers reliable? They are the blood of your business, and they can't be unreliable!

14.   Well-defined target market: This is crucial both for your business and for SEO. If you know exactly who your target market is, you can focus your SEO efforts to put yourself in front of those very people - otherwise you may find that you are chasing the wrong people. In a later chapter, we'll be talking about creating content - you'll see that knowing your customer will help you create the right kind of content.

15.   Potential for growth: Does the way you are building your business allow for growth? When you suddenly get a flood of traffic and orders, will you be able to keep up? This is something you need to consider.

Finally, for something quantifiable, your niche should be getting a decent amount of searches per month! When I started my fish finder store, I did a quick check on the Google Keyword Planner tool(coming up shortly) and saw that "fish finder" received nearly 9,000 searches per month in the United States. That's a pretty decent market size.

This was just one keyword, of course. If you total all the keywords you can target - like blue widget, green widget, widget for widgeting, and other keywords that you can dig up(how to do that is coming right up), you should have a pretty large and decent number.

There's no upper or lower limit, but you'd like to get at least 5,000 visits per month from all your traffic. Assuming you can get 5,000 visits per month(which is on the lower end of the traffic scale), and you can convert that traffic at 1%, that's 50 sales per month, or a little more than 1.5 per day.

At this point, you'll have to ask yourself whether 50 sales per month is worth your while! This will depend on how much your product can make per order.

Of course, 5,000 is incredibly low, and you'll want to aim for much, much more traffic. There is no shortage of keywords and ways to get traffic, but this is the absolute worst case scenario.

Two to three word keyword phrases are like "atomic clocks," "portable solar panels," or "backup mobile batteries." These are a little easier to rank for, and their search volumes are usually in the thousands.

Finally, you have keywords that are longer - phrases and questions. These keywords get searched for very few times a month, but are a lot less competitive. This is where your products and informational pages(resources and blog posts) fall in. If you have 100 products, with each product keyword getting 100 searches per month, that's 10,000 potential customers right there.

The same thing would apply to blog posts - and this is where you can really shine.

Finally, there are variant keywords, the new and unique searches that Google picks up every day. You have no control over these, but as long as your keyword research was solid for the keywords that Google has in their database, you will(should) show up for related and variant keywords too.

Brainstorming for keywords and getting traffic estimates

Brainstorming for keywords is pretty simple. There are two ways to about it.

The first way is to just sit with a blank document and think about what your potential customer would type into Google to find what you are selling, and make a list of those words. You can also use a mind map or a word cloud if that helps you think more clearly.

I also like to use Word Associations to see words related to my main keyword, as well as Google Correlate, which shows you what things Google thinks are related to your keywords.

Once you've come up with this basic list of keywords off the top of your head, it's off to your favorite keyword research tool to help you validate that data.

My two keyword research tools of choice are the Google Keyword Planner(free) and Long Tail Pro(Paid, $97).

To use the Google Keyword Planner, you're going to have to set up an Adwords account using your Google account - it's free.

Under "Find New Keywords", click on "Search for new keywords using a phrase, website, or category"

In the box below, enter your main keyword(don't enter a long tail keyword just yet), and change any settings below - you want to make sure you are targeting the correct country, and under "Keyword Options", try searching once with "Broadly related keyword ideas" and once with "Only show ideas closely related to my search terms."

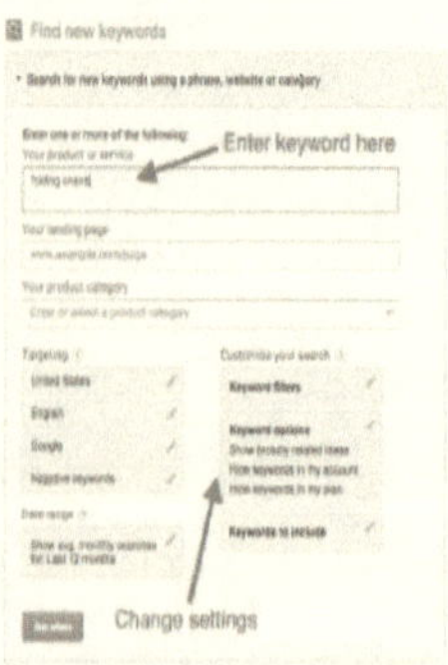

Then click "Get Ideas" and you'll be taken to a page where Google shows you a whole lot of keywords which it feels is related to yours.

Before you start going through the keywords, make sure the "Keyword Ideas" tab is selected, and **not** "Ad Group ideas".

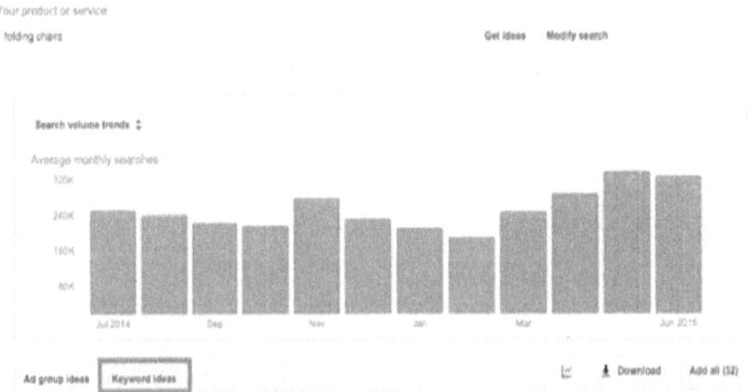

In the "Keyword Ideas" tab, you'll see a table with a handful of columns. The first column is the actual keyword itself, and the next column is "Average Monthly Searches", which is self explanatory.

Keyword (by relevance)	Avg. monthly searches	Competition	Suggested bid	Ad impr. share	Add to plan
folding chair	6,600	High	$1.94	–	
foldable chairs	1,900	High	$2.40	–	
fold up chairs	1,300	High	$1.68	–	
outdoor folding chairs	2,900	High	$1.77	–	
cheap folding chairs	2,400	High	$1.68	–	
folding chairs for sale	1,600	High	$2.22	–	
padded folding chairs	2,400	High	$3.93	–	

In my experience, I've seen that Google tends to lowball this number a little bit - the actual numbers vary in how much more they are than what Google shows.

Note that these keywords are the *exact keywords* that are being used - so if "folding chairs" gets 33,000 searches a month, that's for the exact query "folding chairs", nothing else.

The next columns are "Competition" and "Suggested bid". This competition is **not** SEO competition - it is how many people are advertising for that keyword - so even if you see something that says high competition, don't get disheartened - it's not for SEO. "Suggested bid" is also for advertising - it's what Google recommends you be willing to pay for one click.

The Google Keyword Planner is a great tool, but it's rather clunky and slow, and it's difficult to process large numbers of keywords at once. That's why I prefer using Long Tail Pro - it's an investment, but it's worth it.

There's also another really neat trick that Brian Dean has come up with - and that's to enter your competitor's website in the Google Keyword Planner where it says "Your website" - this way Google will show you a whole bunch of newer ideas that it thinks your competitors *should* be going after, but aren't!

If you've already got a website that you've submitted to Google Webmaster Tools, you can go to the "Search Analytics" tab and you'll see a whole list of keywords that you currently show up for - look for keywords you are ranking for, but don't necessarily have content focused around(and so aren't getting that many clicks), and build content for those keywords.

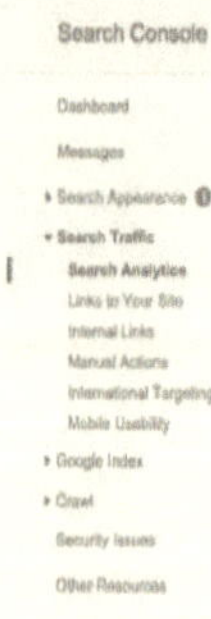

Compiling your keywords and prioritizing

You probably won't find all of your keywords in one go - try with a handful of different keywords from your original list and see how many you can come up with.

Once you've got a huge excel file of your keywords, it's time to compile and prioritize them.

Remember, target one keyword(or two/three similar ones at the most) per page.

For example, a title tag such as "Buy Archery Equipment Online" will be good enough for itself, "Buy Archery Equipment", and "Archery Equipment". Make note, though, that "Buy" makes it a shopping keyword, so a store may receive precedence, whereas "Archery Equipment" is more of a research keyword, so an informational site may receive more preference there.

Again, this is all just speculation based on experience - some of your rankings may happen by accident, and some may be very targeted - it all depends on the Google god - all we can do is really set ourselves up for success.

So your home page will have your main keyword in the title. You can divide up your categories according to sub-keywords, and then build content pages and blog posts around the other long tail keywords. Your product pages will be the product name itself, which is usually a keyword by itself.

Don't really worry too much about how many searches a particular keyword gets *unless* it's your main keyword - the main keyword's searches can be a good gauge for how big a market is.

If your long tail keywords get only 50 or so searches per month, it's fine - 10 blog posts targeting 50 searches per month each is 500 visitors per month, plus there's the unique queries that simply can't be accounted for.

How many keywords? And where?

While there is no hard and fast rule about how many keywords you should have, it's better to have fewer keywords and be more readable than have too many keywords and seem spammy.

You *must* have your target keyword in the title tag, and some people like to put the keyword once or twice in the first paragraph of text. You can also disperse the keyword a few times throughout the entire text.

If there are other very similar keywords that don't warrant an individual page, you can disperse them through the content body as well, to cover your bases.

Use keywords where proper in headings, too.

Measuring competitiveness

Once you've found some good keywords, it's time to see how competitive they are. As we saw earlier, shorter, more concise keywords are usually more competitive, and longer, more specific keywords are usually less competitive.

Even if your primary keyword(folding chairs, to continue the example) is very competitive, there is a LOT of scope for you to go after long-tail keywords to create content around and drive traffic. So don't get disheartened from the first go unless and until you find out that even most of the long tail keywords you come up with are highly competitive.

To measure keyword competitiveness, have a look at the top 10 results on Google. You don't need to pay attention to *how many* pages Google pulls up in total - all you should care about is the top 10 results.

Here's how you should analyze the top 10 results.
Look at:

- The titles of the pages - are they an exact match for your keyword? If so, these people are specifically targeting ranking for that keyword. If not, then there is an opportunity for you.
- The kinds of pages that are ranking - are they all Amazon, About.com, Popular Mechanics, and the like? Huge, super-popular websites that everyone knows about? If so, things are looking tough. If the results are smaller websites(like ones specific to their own niches), then there is a chance you can outrank them with a little time and effort.
- The quality of the content on those pages - how relevant or useful is the content those websites are providing for that keyword? Is there any scope for you to improve the content or make it better?

The easiest keywords to rank for are those where results are not relevant, and you see lots of forum, Yahoo Answers, and Quora-type results. These keywords are ones that no one has really targeted, and you can rank for them with minimal effort.

You also need to size up how big the niche-specific websites are. Just visiting the site can give you an idea. If they seem like a huge website with thousands of pages, thousands of social shares, and have been around for years, then you've got a tough nut to crack.

If they are newer websites, have less content, or are less targeted, then things are a little easier.

To do some quantitative research on your competitors, you can pop over to two of my favorite competitive research tools: SimilarWeb and Open Site Explorer.

SimilarWeb will give you traffic estimates and where that traffic seems to be coming from.

Open Site Explorer will show you Domain Authority(DA) and Page Authority(PA). Domain Authority and Page Authority are metrics developed by Moz. Generally, the higher these two numbers are, the more worthy they are in Google's eyes.

I also like to consult MajesticSEO's Trust Flow and Citation Flow - they are good metrics to see how good of a link profile a site has. Generally, decent sites will have Trust Flows and Citation Flows of at least 10 or more.

I like to see DA under 30 - this is usually something that can be outranked with some work. DA30 and above are established sites and will be harder to outrank.

Then there's PA. PA is weighted off of how many links an individual page has pointing to it(amongst other factors) - so a very low PA is easy to outrank, whereas a high PA will be difficult.

It's also important to consider **relevance**. A targeted site with targeted content is far more likely to rank than a broad site with broad content - so if you see results from big websites that are rather general in nature, you can still go after them with a specific site - provided you can build enough authority for it(more on that in the section on Off-Page SEO).

Note

One mistake I made while starting out was trying to get ALL my pages to rank for my main keyword. Bad idea. Focus on targeting one main keyword per page, and once you have authority and are ranking, you will start to show for the unique searches as well.

Competition research is quite time consuming, as you can see. To check the results and DA/PA for each and every result from the top 10 for multiple keywords is quite tedious and cumbersome. Long Tail Pro makes life a lot easier, since you can just click on a keyword in the interface and it will pull all this data up for you to just eyeball and analyze in a jiffy.

Part 2: On-Page SEO

Now that you have a nice list of keywords, you need to put all of these keywords to use! For that, you need to make sure that your website is properly structured - so that each page leads into the next one properly, and each page is only focused on one particular keyword - so that multiple pages on your own site don't end up competing for the same spot!

Designing a website's structure properly is crucial for good SEO, and it is the first step you need to take.

Site architecture

The way you design your site is also called site architecture. Most of the information that you will find on site architecture is incredibly technical, but for our purposes of an ecommerce store, knowing a few basics is good enough.

When designing any website, you have to make sure that your pages are properly linked together. Sometimes you may end up with an orphaned page, which is basically a page that is a part of your website, but there is no way to access it because no other pages have linked to it!

When a search engine sees your site, a piece of software called a *spider* "crawls" your entire website. It will see whatever text and information is on a particular page, and it will follow any links on that page to other pages - it doesn't matter whether or not these links are to pages on your own site or on outside sites.

This way, the spider gradually "crawls" each and every page on your site, and if the search engine likes what it sees, it will add it to its *index*, which is its database of websites.

Understanding link juice

A factor that has a strong impact on how well your website ranks is how many relevant links your website has from other relevant websites. You can think of a link as a vote of confidence from one site for another. Following this logic, the more links a website has pointing to it, the better the website must be, right?

Yes and no.

When Google started using links as the main determining factor for ranking pages, people started abusing the system and started building millions of trashy links to their pages left and center. Eventually, Google got smart, and now, only relevant and sensible links count - if you have too many trashy links, Google may punish you and remove your site from their index.

Coming back to site architecture, when you get a link from an outside site, you basically get that site's vote and the vote of all the other sites that linked to that site as well! Of course, the juice will be diluted, because link juice flows across all links on a particular page.

Similarly, you can use links to divert link juice internally as well. For most websites, the home page receives a bulk of the links coming to it from outside sites, right? From your home page, you want to link to your category pages, so the link juice flows from home => category. The bulk of the link juice will now be split up, with a little bit going to each category.

From category pages, you will link to product pages, so whatever portion of link juice each category got will now be further diluted onto each product page that is accessible from the category.

This neat graphic does a great job of explaining how it works:

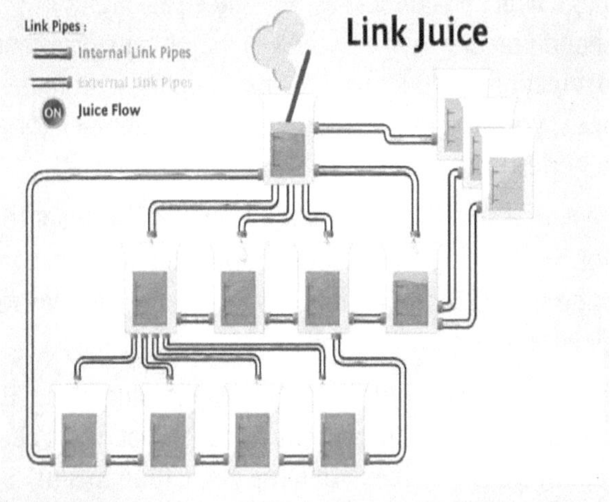

This is only to help you get an understanding of how link juice works.

In a real life example, your home page isn't going to be the *only* page that gets links, so you can actually use any page that gets a lot of links and point to other pages you want to rank from there.

The diagram you saw above is pretty over-simplified, and realistically, instead of link juice flowing in just one direction, it will be going all over the place!

Shopping cart architecture

For the most part, all hosted shopping carts and even open source carts will have similar structure out of the box. The home page will link out to category pages and maybe a few featured products, as well as informational pages and a blog if you have one.

The category pages will not *just* link to product pages, though. Since most ecommerce sites have a navigation menu, every page will link to the home page(through the logo), and all the pages that you decide to link to from the navigation.

This is where things get a little tricky with ecommerce!

On a regular blog, there are only a handful of links in the navigation menu - on an ecommerce store, there are usually tens, if not hundreds! This is just something you have to live with in ecommerce. Some store themes also have a lot of footer links which point to the same pages as the navigation.

You can either keep those, or remove them and design a new footer, it's up to you. Once a page receives a link from any page, any more links to the same page won't be counted as link-juice passing.

A good practice is to only link to major categories and major pages from the navigation. If you have one big category with multiple subcategories, you can try linking out only to major categories and linking to the subcategories from those.

In the end, it's all about *usability*. You NEVER want to sacrifice usability for SEO. Google is getting smarter and smarter, so while it's a good idea to design with Google in mind, it's an even better idea to design with *your customer* in mind.

So if you feel that linking to just major categories will make it harder for your customer to use your website, ignore what I said above and stick in all the categories that you need to in the navigation menu!

Setting up a sitemap

A sitemap is a file that helps search engines make sense of your website. A sitemap is in fact a "map" - just like a map helps you get around your city and shows you where everything is, a sitemap shows search engines what's in your website(all the different pages and sections), and it helps them navigate the whole website and index it quicker.

You can generate a sitemap using a free online tool such as this, use a Wordpress plugin, and most shopping cart software has a sitemap feature built in.

Once you have your sitemap, you can submit it to Google Webmaster Tools and Bing Webmaster Tools. There has been some debate whether or not having a sitemap necessarily improves rankings or not, but it certainly doesn't negatively affect them.

Since a sitemap *does* help search engines crawl your site, you may as well submit one.

Understanding HTML tags

Meta tags are little snippets of code that tell search engines what a particular page is about. The three main types of meta tags are the title, description, and keywords tag. Hosted shopping carts will let you modify these tags without any extra coding.

Title: This is the most crucial tag, and I can't stress its importance enough. The title tag of a page is like the title of a book - it has to be relevant and what your potential readers are looking for! By including your target keywords in your title tags, you are telling search engines that your page is about so and so keyword. Don't take them lightly! This is the most important part of on-page SEO - and has a direct influence on how well you rank for a keyword. A good title tag will also have your company name in it - put it in the beginning if you are well known, or in the end if you are a smaller company.

Description: The description tag is like your advertisement. You have 140 characters to put up a value proposition and get people to click on YOUR listing rather than others. Descriptions influence Click-Thru-Rates, and don't have much of an effect on rankings. They can still make or break your SEO, because you could rank for a keyword at #1, but if no one clicks on your listing, what's the point?

Keywords: The keywords tag is more of a relic from the olden days of SEO where you could stuff a bunch of keywords in this tag and magically rank for them. Search engines are much smarter now, so they don't rely on this tag as much as they used to - or so they tell us. It might be worth putting one or two keywords for a page, which can be an extra nudge - a sort of *hint*hint* to Google and Yahoo. Don't stuff a bunch of keywords under any circumstances, though!

The three types of tags we saw are overall tags. There is one other set of HTML tags you can use to help make more sense of your page's content to both search engines and people.

Heading tags: Heading tags are self explanatory - you want to use them to start off a new section on your page. For example, the name of the blog post or the name of the product is usually wrapped in an H(eading)1 tag, which is a very broad and overall heading. Putting your keyword into an H1 tag is a good hint to search engines what your page is about.

Then you have other heading tags from H2 all the way to H6. I've never used anything less than an H4, and that also on very long pages. Most of the time, H1, H2, and H3 tags will suffice.

It's a good idea to split your posts, pages, and product descriptions into subsections. Start each subsection with an H2 tag describing what the section is about. If a subsection was long enough to warrant subsections of its own, then you want to start those off with H3 tags.

Your page should end up looking something like this:

```
<h1>Your main keyword</h1>
<h2>Subheading one</h2>
Content....
<h2>Subheading two</h2>
Content...
<h3>Sub-subheading one</h3>
Content...
<h2>Subheading three</h2>
Content...
...and so on
```

By splitting your page up like this, not unlike the different sections of this book, you make it easier for people to skim through your page, and also for search engines to better categorize and index your website.

Optimizing images

Don't underestimate the power of image searches - you might be surprised at how many people find you through images and not pages themselves. There are two things you want to do with any images you put on your store's pages - give them a good filename and assign good alt text.

Alt text is the little snippet of text you see when an image fails to load. Since search engines cannot see images, they look for alt text in images to try and figure out what that image is about. So if you had an image of a large green whackamole machine, you'd want to set the alt text to say something to that effect. Most hosted carts like Shopify and BigCommerce both have an in-built option for entering alt text.

The filename should also be sensible, like a model number(if that's how people find your product) or the product itself - green-whackamole-machine.jpg.

Redirects

Redirects are lines of code that tell search engines where to go(or what happened to a page). The most important redirect you need to know and implement where necessary is a **301 redirect**.

A 301 redirect tells search engines that this page has moved to a new address, and forwards them to that new address.

So if you had http://archeryproshop.io/bow-and-arrow-for-kids-under-20/ and wanted to change the URL to /bow-and-arrow-kids/ without losing the rankings that the original URL had, you'd set up a redirect from that old URL to the new one, and move the page to the new URL.

Now, any links still pointing to the old URL from other websites will now automatically go to the new URL.

Not only can you do this on your own site, but from entirely different sites, too - which is an invaluable tool when you are switching domains or moving from one platform to another.

When I switched my old store which was hosted on Bigcommerce on to Wordpress as an Amazon affiliate site, all my URLs changed, so I set up a redirect for every old URL to a new URL on the Wordpress site. Because of this, my rankings were not affected.

You can also use redirects when you take down a page(such as for a discontinued product), but don't want that page's SEO value to disappear, so you can redirect that page to any other page of your choosing.

Adding Schema.org markup

Schema.org markup is special HTML code that you can add to your product and category pages to show extra information in Google search results.

For example, when you search for certain products, some store results show with a little extra text such as "17 products". That is because the store has implemented Schema.org markup.

Steam Mops | BISSELL
www.bissell.com › ... › Browse by Type › Steam & Hard Floor Cleaners ▾
10 Results - BISSELL® steam mops leave your hard floors squeaky clean & can be ready to go in as little ... Forget your mops & buckets; find your steam mop today.

For product pages, Schema.org markup can show the number of reviews, the review stars, and the price, and if it is in stock or not, all in the search results. This greatly helps in increasing the number of clicks on search results.

Apple iPhone 6 Plus | Verizon Wireless
www.verizonwireless.com › Smartphones › Apple ▾
★★★★⯪ Rating: 4.6 - 7,358 reviews - US$ 31.24 - In stock
The iPhone 6 Plus from Apple boasts a sleek design and Touch ID fingerprint sensor.
Choose from Gold, Gray, or Silver phone colors. Read customer reviews.

Best Practices For Your Pages

Best practices for home pages

It is highly likely that you are going to target your main keyword from your home page, so your home page of all places shouldn't be devoid of content!

Have a look at Binoculars.com, which is a Hayneedle store. After their main splash image and featured products, they have **content**.

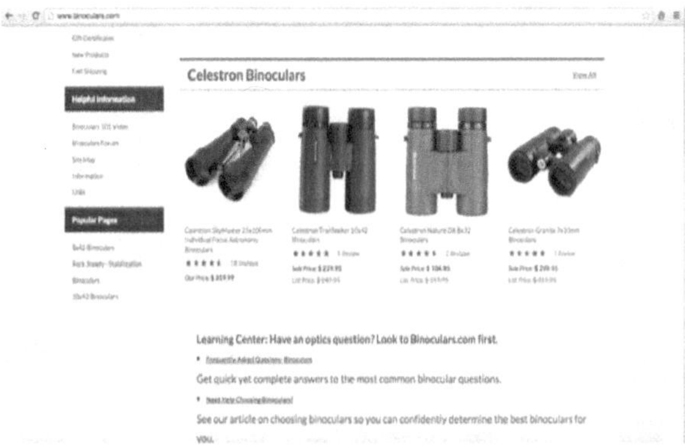

Now it doesn't really matter if your content comes at the top of the page or the bottom(it's usually going to be at the bottom, since the top will be reserved for images) - you just have to have some high quality content that provides real value to your customers.

Also, like you saw in the section on optimizing images, make sure your home page images have good titles, filenames, and good ALT text - if a picture is worth a 1000 words, Google should know about it!

Not literally a 1000 words.

But you get the point - there should be at least a few sentences to one paragraph on your home page image ALT texts, and it should be *original* content.

Best practices for category pages

Category pages should be treated the same way as home pages. Since most category pages are just a list of products, add a helpful introduction the the top of your category pages describing the category and helping your customer make a more informed decision.

Depending on the shopping cart you have, you may not have control over your thumbnail ALT text, so having good category content is crucial - it doesn't have to be really long, but just relevant.

One problem with having too long category page content is that it'll throw your customers off - they came in expecting products, and instead they got a blog post - so find the best balance.

Have a look at TrollingMotors.net's category pages:

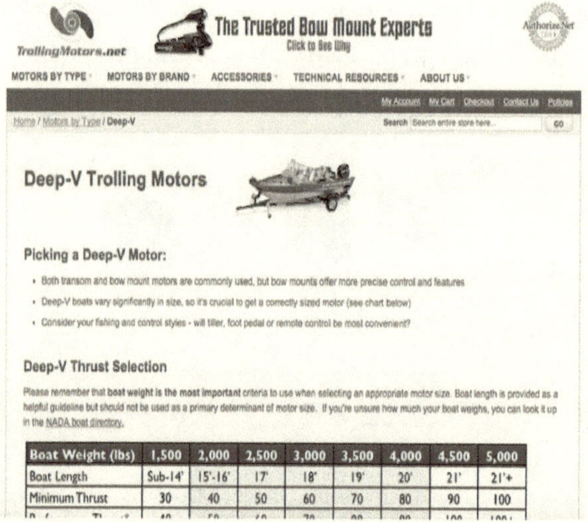

Boat Weight (lbs)	1,500	2,000	2,500	3,000	3,500	4,000	4,500	5,000
Boat Length	Sub-14'	15'-16'	17'	18'	19'	20'	21'	21'+
Minimum Thrust	30	40	50	60	70	80	90	100

Best practices for product pages

Your product pages are where you should really let your content shine. Don't limit your product descriptions - give them flair and personality, and most importantly, make them nice and lengthy as far as possible.

Treat each individual product page like a blog post - don't leave anything on the table. If a customer wants to research a product, they need to be able to find whatever information they need all on your product page.

This includes embedding images - I like to use them in the description, too, along with the main product images - and videos, too. This is not so much for a direct SEO benefit, but it does have an indirect effect, since the more time you can get people to spend on your pages, the more "worthy" those pages will look to Google.

A lower bounce rate will also help, since bounce rate is one of the factors Google considers in ranking a page.

For learning how to write the best product descriptions, I like to learn from the masters of ecommerce - Amazon - and see how they write descriptions for their prize product, the Kindle.

You may not be able to get the same formatting as Amazon does, but you can see how they use long-form content, and split up the product description into paragraphs and sub-sections using headings.

They also use lots and lots of rich media - images, videos, and beautiful arrangement. Go all out with your product descriptions - especially the ones that get the most traffic. You want to make your product pages so good that your customers don't have to go anywhere else - you've answered every question imaginable!

Remember, treat each product description like a blog post!

Using Webmaster Tools

To manage your online store's search presence and make sure everything is running smoothly, you should set up your store in Google Webmaster Tools and Bing Webmaster Tools.

By adding your site, these tools will show you how many pages from your site are indexed, how many errors your sitemap is throwing(when it says a page should be there but there is none), how many search clicks you are getting per month, and to an extent, which keywords you are currently getting clicks for.

To set up Google Webmaster Tools, head over there, and log in with a Google account. It's a good idea to have a separate account for your store.

Then click the red "Add a property" button on the top right, and enter your site's address in the bar that pops up, and continue.

You will then have to verify that you own this website - Google suggests a couple of methods of doing so, and they are all quite straightforward.

Once you are verified, you will be taken to the dashboard, and you are all set! Click around and explore the different features they give you. It will probably take a few weeks before you start seeing some real data.

You can also set up the same site on <u>Bing Webmaster Tools</u>, too.

Part 3: Off-Page SEO

All of the on-page optimization in the world can only take you so far without off-page SEO. Off-page SEO is the hard part, but it really pays.

There used to be a time where it was as easy as simply blasting links to your site from all over the web - nowadays, that will get you penalized and removed from Google's index quicker than you can say "backlinks".

The best way to do off-page SEO is to create solid content and then promote the hell out of it.

SEO has evolved more from being simply SEO to "content marketing" and "relationship building".

Content marketing and networking

The thought behind content marketing is that with great content, links will come automatically. While that *is* true to a certain extent, it won't happen by itself - you will *have* to promote your content, or else how will anyone see it?

There are two ways of going about your content strategy. Depending on your niche, you'll either be able to implement one of them, or both.

The first way is to create very in-depth resources about the details of your product and how to use it. I mean go *all out*. Create resources that blow forum posts out of the water, and leave nothing wanting for the customer.

Some examples of this content are installation guides, buying guides, usage guides, technical specifications, compatibility guides, and the like.

This is the same strategy Andrew Youderian used on Right Channel Radios. By creating such great resources, coupled with some link building, he managed to rank very high for a lot of these technical search queries, and as a result, his traffic grew, and he had overall happier customers, too.

SELECTION GUIDES

Covers the most popular antennas, radios and mounting locations for pickup trucks. Everything you need to know to get a CB up and running in your truck.

CHOOSING THE BEST CB RADIO

Everything you need to know to get a CB installed in your CJ, classic Wrangler or JK. Covers the most popular antennas, radios and mounting locations for Jeeps.

CHOOSING THE BEST CB ANTENNA

Of course, not all niches will have technical products where a lot of content can be created around the product itself, like housewares and other simple items.

At that point, you'll have to go with strategy number 2, which is to create content that *someone using your product would find useful.*

Ezra Firestone from Smart Marketer has done a great job with this strategy for the store he runs, <u>Boom! By Cindy Joseph</u>.

BBCJ sells cosmetic and skin care products for older women. You can see how there probably isn't much interesting stuff to be said about the product itself, but Ezra drives an incredible amount of traffic and brand awareness using content marketing.

BBCJ creates content that appeals to their customers - older women. So on their vlog(they use video, another very powerful content form), you'll find beauty and health tips that are tailored to older women.

You can see how this form of content marketing is very powerful - it is not salesy at all, and it is something that their customers find very relatable and very useful - so they will be more likely to share it, and they actually don't mind - *even look forward to* - receiving new content from BBCJ!

So if you feel there is not much to write about your product itself, think about who would most likely use your product, and create content they would find useful.

It will be easier for some niches than for others, but with a little experimentation, you should be able to find out what works and what doesn't.

The best way to experiment is to create some content, promote it, and see what kind of a response you get - do people share the content? Do they like it? Do they comment on it? This will help you gauge it.

If you are wondering at this point *how* you are going to promote your content, that's a very good question!

Creating and promoting your content

The first step to promote your content is to create content that is promotion-worthy.

It's better to create less content and promote it more than to create more content and promote it less. So you don't even need to have a dedicated blog - you can even just have a few solid resource pages that you can promote over and over again, and once it reaches a tipping point, it'll be the gift that keeps on giving.

So what kind of content should you create?

From the earlier section, we've already listed solid resource pages and informational pages about your product.

Some more content ideas are:

Infographics: Infographics are great because they have shareability built into them. Everyone loves a good image, and people are very likely to share images, especially on social media sites like Facebook and Pinterest.

To build an infographic, think about what data is related to your product/niche/audience. Dig up that data, present it in a visual way(or get a designer to do it - you'll find plenty of infographic designers on Fiverr or Elance). You can also use an online service like Vengage.

To get some inspiration for an infographic, you can head over to Google and do a quick search for "your niche infographic" to see what other people have already made - then you can either improve what is already there, or use that as inspiration for a new angle.

Once your infographic is ready, go back to the Google results and see where those infographics have been posted or shared - and approach those website owners and simply ask if they'd like to share your infographic!

Expert roundups: Expert roundups are like infographics but on steroids. That's because while you have to go and ask people to share your infographic, the experts you feature on your expert roundup will share the post themselves!

To create an expert roundup, you need to first think of a good question that you want these experts to answer. For example, one of the roundups I did here was around the question "What is the weirdest link you have ever built for a store?"

You will need to think up a similar question related to your niche or audience.

Then, to simplify things, head over to Google, and see what expert roundups have already been done related to your niche! This will help in two ways: first to make sure you aren't repeating what's already been done, and second, by parsing a few roundups, you'll have a ready list of experts to approach that you *know* participate in these roundups!

More content ideas: To see what kind of content does really well in your niche, head over to BuzzSumo and search using your niche as the main keyword. You can get some data for free, but for more in-depth results, you will need to sign up for a paid account.

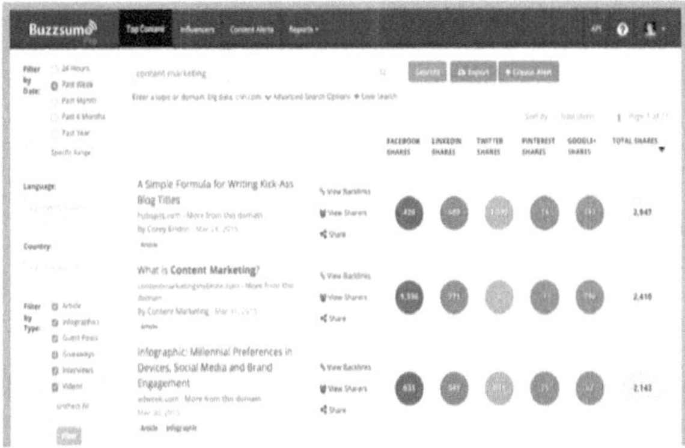

You can search any topic in BuzzSumo, and see how many shares and backlinks popular posts around those topics received. You can also filter by time and type of content.

Once you know what is trending, *make it better*. Then go to "View sharers", and approach them to share your new, improved content!

Link building

Link building was and still is an incredibly important part of search engine optimization. You can have the best content in the world, but without good links, you simply can't rank for even a mildly competitive keyword.

Not all links are created equal, though, so here is a rundown of the types of links there are and what they can do for you.

Broadly speaking, links are of two types: *do-follow* and *no-follow*.

Do-follow links are links that literally tell search engine spiders(remember them?) to *follow* the link to whatever site it goes to. A do-follow link is a link that passes its vote to the next website, guiding the search engine spider from itself to the other site.

Examples of do-follow links are blog post mentions, infographic links, resource links, and most usual scenarios where one site links to another.

No-follow links are links that do the opposite. When a search engine spider reaches a no-follow link, it simply sees the link, but does not follow it to the website it points to. It simply moves on, so that website doesn't *really* get the other website's vote.

Examples of no-follow links are blog comments, forum links, and links from social media profiles.

The whole concept of no-follow links probably came about because people realized in the early days of SEO that they could game the system and just build a ton of links using blog comments and forum spam, and get themselves ranked high in Google, who at that time put a lot of weight on just links in general.

A natural backlink profile is one that has a healthy mix of **both** do-follow and no-follow links. Usually there will be more do-follow links, and fewer no-follow links, but it's always good to have both.

Another important thing to remember in link building is **anchor text**.

Anchor text is the actual part of the text that links to the other page. On most websites, for example, all anchor text is colored in blue. On other websites, it may be a different color.

In the early days of SEO, anchor text was all Google had to see what the other site being linked to was about. So a link with the anchor text "archery equipment" would probably be to a site about, you guessed it, archery equipment! Again, it's not that simple, because people could really easily game the system.

That's why Google came out with an update called Penguin that cracked down on sites that built links to themselves using spammy tactics, and one of the things it looked at was anchor text. So a healthy link profile today would be one that would have varied anchor text - not just anchor text optimized using keywords.

You *can* still use keywords, and you *should*, but not just that - a good idea is to include a phrase that has your keyword or part of it in itself as the entire anchor text, for example, "good places to buy archery equipment here", instead of just "archery equipment" or "buy archery equipment".

You also want to have some natural anchor text, such as "click here", or "read more", as well as naked URLs, like "http://archeryproshop.io", or whatever your website is.

Note: Sometimes, you will find that your content has been copied entirely on other sites(as syndication), or you have multiple copies of the same content on different pages of your site. To make sure search engines don't consider this to be duplicate content, you can add a rel="canonical" tag in your duplicate(and original) pages like this:

<link rel="canonical" href="https://store.example.com/widgets/green-widgets-are-awesome" />

This will tell search engines where the original content can be found.
Getting links

Guest posting: Guest posting is one of the best ways to get your website in front of thousands of interested visitors and get a few good links out of the whole process.

The key to finding good guest posting opportunities is tied into who your ideal customer is, something that you would have researched as you were choosing your niche. Once you know your ideal customer, it's only a matter of finding out where they like to hang out.

Most probably this will be around the blogs and websites of large influencers in your niche.

A simple Google search for "widget blog" or "industry blog" will show you some great results. You can also go to Alltop.com and find blogs there.

When looking for blogs, don't just focus on the HUGE ones, as those are probably going to be the least likely to entertain a new small business. Focus on medium sized and smaller ones. You'll still put yourself in front of a good audience and you'll still get a good link.

Make a list of all the blogs you find, and start reaching out to them.

The topic you choose to write about can be anything. It doesn't necessarily have to be directly related to the product - it just has to be something your target customer finds relevant.

In the guest post, you can link out to relevant products/pages on your website - but don't link *only* to your site - link out to other sites as well. This makes the post seem more genuine and less like something crafted solely for the purpose of a link.

Doing outreach

A very large part of your SEO and link building success will depend greatly on how good you are at doing outreach to potential link prospects. A lot has been said about how to write great outreach emails, so I'm going to keep it short here and put some recommended reads at the bottom of this section.

When doing outreach, I like to make a Google Spreadsheet to keep track of who I have emailed and how far each lead has progressed. This prevents me from sending duplicate emails too soon, and just lets me see the progress in an organized way.

A few factors make a good outreach email:

Making it about *them*: Instead of asking for a favor, a good outreach email will point out what is in it for the blog/website/influencer that you are approaching. So don't just say you want a guest post, but point out how a guest post about a certain topic will be a good fit for their blog and why that blog's audience will appreciate it.

Keeping it short: Most of the people you will be looking to approach probably get a boatload of emails every day. If an email is too much effort to read, they just may not read it. Keep your email short, sweet, and to the point.

Making it personal: Nobody pays much attention to an email if it was just a random CC using a boilerplate message. Show that you've actually read that person's website or blog, and throw in a small compliment at the beginning of the message. If not a compliment, offer an alternative viewpoint on something they wrote(but be nice). A single line like this does wonders to grab someone's attention.

Knowing how to ask: It is a lot easier to get the link once you have established a relationship with the blogger instead of doing a hard sell. Focus on using the first email or so on building a relationship, and use the next few emails to pitch your idea - even if you introduced it in the first email. Once someone has read your email and replied to you, chances that they'll read and reply again are very high, so that's when you want to make your pitch.

That being said, sometimes it is better to say what you want in the first email. It will depend on situation to situation, and unfortunately, there is no set of rules that can really help you decide when to do a hard sell and when to open a conversation.

Aside from that, nailing outreach is all about practice, practice, and more practice. It's unlikely that there will be a shortage of websites in your niche, so even if you screw up a few emails, there will always be another site. Plus, what's to say you can't approach an influencer again in the future and get a response then?

If they didn't read your email before, they probably won't remember you. ;)

Some websites make it notoriously difficult to find contact information. If they don't have a form or don't display their email address, there are still some other ways to get in touch.

The fastest way is using Twitter if they have an account. Simple tweet at them with your request and ask them either for their email address or give them yours.

If that doesn't work, or they don't use Twitter, then there is a sneaky way to find emails.

Pop over to http://www.whois.com/whois and enter the domain name of the person you are trying to contact. If they haven't sealed their information, you will be able to see their contact details - voila! You now have an email address to work with!

Copying your competitors' links

A really nice way to get a good bunch of links without having to scour around too much is to simply see where your competitors have been getting their links, and get links from there.

It's highly doubtful that you can copy *all* their links, but you should be able to get quite a few - especially low hanging fruit links like directory submissions. These won't have as much value, but they are still links.

You'll also be able to see where they got their editorial mentions, and you'll see that those websites mention other stores, so that will make them more viable outreach targets.

To see where your competitors are getting links, use a tool like Open Site Explorer, Majestic SEO, or Ahrefs. I like Majestic SEO or Ahrefs rather than Open Site Explorer, because those two have far larger indices than OSE, and you'll just be able to see a lot more links from them.

Simply go over to Ahrefs, OSE, or Majestic SEO, create a free account, and plug your competitor's domain into the search bar. These tools will spit out all the links your competitors have(that they know of), and you can even download a .csv of the results to save and parse later.

Keep in mind that free accounts will only show you limited results - to see the full results, you'll need to sign up for a paid account.

Directories and manufacturers: Another easy kind of link to get is to find industry and niche directories and submit your site to them. You may have read in some places that directories are bad - and it's not quite the case. Directories are bad if they are spammy and look very obviously spammy!

There are plenty of pages out there on the web whose sole purpose is to help visitors find exactly what they are looking for. Many websites must be out there focused on archery that have a specific page where they link out to good archery supply stores - these are the kinds of pages you want to find and get links from.

Some pages will have a "Submit your site" button, and for others, you will need to go through the contact form to find them.

If you sell products manufactured by another company, simply head over to the manufacturer's website and there is a very good chance that they'll have a "where to buy" page. This is another good place to get your website listed. Again, use the contact form.

When emailing a manufacturer, send a professional email, show them your site, why you are serious about selling their product, and the supplier you are getting it from - this will help show you mean business - but keep it short and sweet, too.

Broken links: Old websites die, and new websites come up. Such is the law of the internet. Luckily for us, the links pointing to old websites don't always die with them. So at any point, there are millions of links out there pointing to websites that don't exist anymore.

Searching around websites in your niche(especially directory pages and links pages) will reveal some links that are pointing to dead pages. These are broken links.

Now all you have to do is replicate the dead page(which you can see what it looked like by heading over to http://www.archive.org and using the "Wayback Machine"), make it a little better, and then approach the site owner with the broken link and suggest your new, improved resource.

Social Media

Utilizing social media is another good way to drive traffic for difficult keywords. Your site may not have enough authority and links to rank for a particular keyword, but a social media site sure will! So many results in Google are from Facebook and Pinterest - so if you can build a Facebook Page or a Pinterest Board around a particular keyword, you may get some good traffic from there, too.

Of course, people will start out by going to your Pinterest or Facebook Page, but hopefully you'll have some links to great content on your own website that people will click through.

I'm not going to go into too much detail on social media at this time, because it's really outside the scope of this guide, and hopefully I will start working on a similar guide for social media platforms, too.

Grey Hat SEO

Grey Hat SEO is entering a little bit into stuff that Google frowns upon, but it can still be used to give your store a quick boost. Please note that *grey hat SEO **should not form the basis of your SEO efforts!** If grey hat is all you do, you are putting your entire business at risk!*

With that disclaimer out of the way, let's get into a neat way you can boost your link juice.

Expired domains: Thousands of domain names expire every day, and many of those thousands used to be prosperous websites, each with a lot of links pointing to them. Chances are, when the website went down, the links didn't. So if you happened to get your hands on these domains, you'd suddenly be sitting on a lot of links, right?

Finding expired domains is very easy.

Finding *good* expired domains isn't. I usually search at expireddomains.net - you can make a free account, and start searching right away. You can enter keywords to search, and they will show you what expired domains have those words, and they'll also show you a bunch of other metrics like backlinks, page rank(though now practically defunct, it's still a good metric to eyeball a domain), Alexa rank, and others.

Remember to be very broad with these searches - using long tail keywords to search here will really limit your results - so go for a broad niche-related keyword.

One thing I find tough about these expired domains is a lot of domains probably expire that we can never find using keywords - because the domains were a proprietary brand, and didn't have any keywords in the domain. But still, with a little searching, you can sometimes uncover some gems.

Now the first page you'll see won't be sorted, and a lot of these domains are going to be junk, so you'll have to apply some filters to narrow down the results.

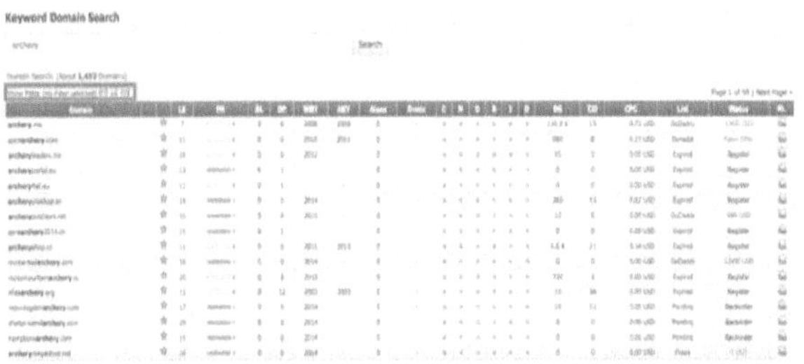

Keyword Domain Search

When you click Show Filter, there will be a lot of options, but I like to set the minimum Page Rank as 1 and minimum backlinks as 1. This will narrow down the results quite a bit, and then you can start perusing the results.

You may not find a good domain every time you search - sometimes the really good domains will be too expensive, sometimes backlink profiles won't check out. It's very hit or miss!

When you do come across a domain that is in your price range, before you go ahead and click the price(which takes you to the auction or buy page), do some quick backlink analysis.

Plug the site into Majestic SEO and check the citation flow and trust flow(which we saw earlier) and make sure they are both higher than at least 10. You also want to scroll down in the Majestic SEO results screen and quickly scan the anchor text to make sure it's not too optimized, and also see where the links are coming from - are they more or less relevant or not?

Otherwise you are looking at a domain someone bought and did black hat SEO on, and that's no good, because you don't want to own something like that.

When you *do* find a good domain, there are a couple of things you can do with it.

Set up a 301 redirect to your main website: If the backlinks are relevant to your site as well, a quick-and-dirty thing you can do is simply add the domain to your own hosting account, and set up a 301 redirect from that domain to any page on your own. Effectively, this will funnel all the link juice coming to that domain directly to yours!

This is a little risky because you never *truly* know what links were built to that domain, so unless you are 100% sure that the links are (mostly) legit and *relevant to your site,* move on to the next method.

Set up an entirely new website on the domain: Since you have a domain with lots of links pointing to it, chances are that it can rank pretty easily for some related keywords, right? So why not build a website on that domain, put up 5-15 good posts on the site, and link out from some of those posts to page on your main website?

This is quite similar to building a PBN, except most PBNs have low quality content - the difference here is you want to make sure the content you put on this new website is *actually useful for people*. You can outsource the content, sure, but it should be useful.

Also, *don't* buy this domain under the same account you own your main domain with, and don't even host it with the same provider, let alone the same account.

When you build links from that site to yours, link out to other people as well - if the entire purpose of a site is just to link to one other site, Google senses that something is up. Link out to multiple websites from your new site's copy.

So this is something you can do when guest posts are difficult to come by. Some niches *will* be harder to write for, no doubt - so this is an option for you if that is the case.

Part 4: Should you hire an SEO agency?

Finally, as this guide comes to a close, let's get into something a lot of us consider every day. Should you hire an SEO agency?

The answer isn't quite as straightforward as you'd like it to be, but in the interest of oversimplification, yes and no.

Yes, if you go with a huge, trusted agency. These guys have proven track records, work with household-name companies, and have too much at stake to mess around with their SEO - and they also cost more than most of us could afford to spend.

No, if you go with a smaller, lesser-known agency, that only claims to do SEO. This is nothing against SEO agencies - it's just that you just don't know what kind of SEO they are going to be doing.

That was the simple answer.

The more detailed answer is that it's very possible that you may well *need* someone else to do SEO because you just don't have the time to do it yourself.

If you have the budget for it, hire a great agency, by all means. In fact, some of the folks who were kind enough to provide their expert opinions are part of SEO agencies.

So how can you vet an agency to make sure they know what they are doing?

For starters, on their home page, check out who their clients are, and where they have been featured.

If they've been featured on big name blogs like Search Engine Land, Moz, and the like, they probably know what they are doing, since those sites won't really feature anything that isn't up to the mark.

You also want to look at what they do, and the types of clients they entertain. Are their clients small niche sites and grey-hat people? Or are their clients real businesses with a lot at stake?

They will also feature testimonials on their websites - it wouldn't hurt to just drop a line to those businesses and ask them how their experience with that company way.

If you don't have such a large budget, there is still a solution.

One way to get around that is to hire someone in-house to do the SEO for you. It's crucial that you yourself know what links are being built, and how your pages are optimized - but you can leave the grunt work and everything up to someone else.

Agencies may not be as timely with their reports, and if you get a report one month later of 1000 shady links, you'll have your work cut out for you.

Another way to do it is to look at it like this. SEO is a lot of things put together, as we've seen so far.

So find the one thing that you are having trouble with, and get a guy(or gal) to help you with that.

If you've got too many products to ever optimize title tags and meta descriptions yourself, get a guy to do that.

If you don't have the time to do guest post outreach and networking, get a guy to do that, and write the posts yourself, so you have control of the content and where they go.

If you don't have time for even that, approve the places your guy gets you a guest post, and get another guy to write the post for you.

If you don't think you are creative, get someone to come up with good content ideas and have them create that content for you.

Do you see where I am going with this? Don't package it all up into "SEO" and hire one company to do it. If you don't have the time, it's understandable, but break it up into bits and get someone to do those bits, but make sure you are the one that assembles them in the end. This way you have full control over what's going on.

The good thing about this method is you can probably outsource some tasks for much cheaper than others, and you'll save some money along the way, too.

Of course, if you've got the budget, by all means, hire a name brand agency to help - they will most probably deliver.

Closing thoughts

SEO is an ongoing process. There is no point in SEO where you can get complacent and think "hmm, I've done enough SEO". If you've got some pages that are ranked high and bring lots of good traffic, what about your other pages? Can you optimize them, build links, and promote them?

The important thing to keep in mind is that SEO is an integral part of your business - not just something you can do on the side. Even if you are getting all of your traffic from other channels like Adwords, those will only bring you traffic as long as you keep pumping money into them.

SEO, when done properly, is the only way to get your business long-lasting traffic and build true value for your site even if you stop paying for traffic from other channels. It's also very passive - so once you are receiving the traffic, you'll keep getting it as long as you aren't outranked.

Nothing on the internet is permanent, that's for sure - but SEO is the damn closest thing to permanency that you can do for your business.

25 Point SEO Checklist

1. Do your keyword research BEFORE you start building your website
2. SEO should be part of the initial design, not an afterthought
3. Organize your site with a logical structure – use categories and subcategories
4. Make sure your title tags have your target keyword in them
5. If you have one main keyword, target it with your homepage, and create separate pages for other target keywords. DO NOT attempt to target too many keywords to one page – it won't work!
6. "Long Tail" keywords are much easier to rank for – these are keywords that have few searches per month, and are much longer, usually multiple word phrases
7. Your title tags should not be longer than 70 characters
8. Your H1 tags should have the keyword in them too
9. Make sure to repeat your keyword a few times throughout your content – this makes it sound relevant to Google
10. Don't overuse your keyword – otherwise it looks spammy!
11. Focus on delivering good, valuable content
12. Write for people, not search engines
13. Try to use different heading tags(h1, h2, h3, h4) to organize your content
14. Studies have shown that longer content(2000 words or greater) tends to rank higher
15. Link out to authority sites – this makes your site look more authentic and genuine
16. Use the "Grandma Rule" when designing any website. Ask yourself: "Would you send Grandma to this site?"
17. Links are like "votes of confidence" by other websites to yours. In general, the more genuine links you have, the better your site

will do.

18.   When you build links, try to vary them(like directories, blog posts, link pages, etc)

19.   Don't overuse anchor text. If you are targeting "large jump ropes" as your keyword, don't make all your links say "large jump ropes." Vary them!

20.   Only get links from sites you wouldn't mind linking to yourself – if it's a crappy site, it's not worth it!

21.   Relevancy is incredibly important with link building. For "large jump ropes," a site about kid's playground activities is a good place to get links. A site about witches cauldrons is not!

22.   Remember to cross-link between pages of your sites, too – and not just by categories – in the content too!

23.   Links work by passing "link juice" from one page to another. If you have a page on your site that has a lot of "link juice," pages you link to from that page will get a part of that "juice."

24.   Be social! A page that has been shared a lot on social networks like Facebook, Twitter, and Google+ will rank higher than others

25.   Give it time! Climbing in rankings is a long process – invest in it well and the payoff will be huge. Don't try to rush things.